عشرة أسباب للوقاية من السحر والعين

TEN PREVENTIVE MEASURES AGAINST

MAGIC AND ENVY

SHAYKH 'ABDUR RAZZĀQ BIN
'ABDUL MUHSIN AL-'ABBĀD AL-BADR

Maktabatulirshad Publications Ltd.

© Maktabatulirshad Publications, USA

All rights reserved. No part of this publication may be reproduced in any language, stored in any retrieval system or transmitted in any form or by any means, whether electronic, mechanic, photocopying, recording or otherwise, without the express permission of the copyright owner.

ISBN: 978-1-9442-4765-2

First Edition: Rabīʿ Awwal 1437 A.H. /January 2016 C.E.

Cover Design: Pario Studio UK
info@pariostudio.com

Translation by Abdullah Omrān

Revision & Editing by Maktabatulirshad staff

Typesetting & formatting by Abū Sulaymān Muhammad "Abdul-Azim Ibn Joshua Baker

Printing: Ohio Printing

Subject: Akhlāq

Website: www.maktabatulirshad.com
E-mail: info@maktabatulirshad.com

CONTENTS

BRIEF BIOGRAPHY OF THE AUTHOR 5

ARABIC SYMBOL TABLE 8

INTRODUCTION 9

THE FIRST MEASURE: TO SEEK REFUGE IN ALLĀH 17

THE SECOND MEASURE: TO HAVE TAQWĀ 21

THE THIRD MEASURE: ENDURING THE HARM OF ONE'S ENEMY 27

THE FOURTH MEASURE: TRUST IN ALLĀH 31

THE FIFTH MEASURE: TO EMPTY THE HEART FROM THINKING 42

THE SIXTH MEASURE: DEVOTION AND SINCERITY TO ALLĀH 47

THE SEVENTH MEASURE: TO FILTER OUT ONE'S REPENTANCE TO ALLĀH FROM ALL SINS 50

THE EIGHTH MEASURE: TO GIVE OUT CHARITY 55

THE NINTH MEASURE: TO SUPPRESS THE BLAZING FURY OF THE ENVIER 59

THE TENTH MEASURE: TO COMPLETELY PURIFY TAWHĪD FOR ALLĀH 63

QUESTIONS 70

TEN PREVENTIVE MEASURES AGAINST MAGIC AND ENVY

BRIEF BIOGRAPHY OF THE AUTHOR

His name: Shaykh 'Abdur Razzāq bin 'Abdul Muhsin al-'Abbād al-Badr.

He is the son of the *'Allāmah* and *Muhaddith* of Medina Shaykh 'Abdul-Muhsin al 'Abbād al-Badr.

Birth: He was born on the 22nd day of *Dhul-Qa'dah* in the year 1382 AH in az-Zal'fi, Kingdom of Saudi Arabia. He currently resides in Medina.

Current Occupation: He is a member of the teaching staff at the Islāmic University of Medina.

Scholastic Certifications: Doctorate in *'Aqīdah*.

BRIEF BIOGRAPHY OF THE AUTHOR

The Shaykh has authored books, researches, as well as numerous explanations in different disciplines. Among them are:

1. *Fiqh of Supplications & adh-Kār.*

2. *Hajj & Refinement of Souls.*

3. Explanation of '*Exemplary Principles*' by Shaykh Ibn 'Uthaymīn (رحمه الله).

4. Explanation of the book, *The Principles of Names & Attributes*, authored by Shaykh-ul-Islām Ibn al-Qayyim (رحمه الله).

5. Explanation of the book, *Good Words*, authored by Shaykh-ul-Islām Ibn al-Qayyim (رحمه الله).

6. Explanation of the book, *al-Aqīdah at-Tahāwiyyah.*

7. Explanation of the book, *Fusūl: Biography of the Messenger*, by Ibn Kathīr (رحمه الله).

TEN PREVENTIVE MEASURES AGAINST MAGIC AND ENVY

8. An explanation of the book, *al-Adab-ul-Mufrad*, authored by Imām Bukhārī (رحمه الله).

From the most distinguished scholars whom he has learned knowledge from are:

1. His father the *'Allāmah* Shaykh 'Abdul Muhsin al-Badr (حفظه الله).

2. The *'Allāmah* Shaykh ibn Bāz (رحمه الله).

3. The *'Allāmah* Shaykh Muhammad Ibn Sālih al-'Uthaymīn (رحمه الله).

4. Shaykh 'Ali Ibn Nāsir al-Faqīhi (حفظه الله).

ARABIC SYMBOL TABLE

Arabic Symbols & their meanings

حفظه الله	May Allāh preserve him
رَضِيَ اللهُ عَنْهُ	(i.e. a male companion of the Prophet Muhammad)
سُبْحَانَهُ وَتَعَالَى	Glorified & Exalted is Allāh
عَزَّوَجَلَّ	(Allāh) the Mighty & Sublime
تَبَارَكَ وَتَعَالَى	(Allāh) the Blessed & Exalted
جَلَّ وَعَلَا	(Allāh) the Sublime & Exalted
عَلَيْهِ الصَّلَاةُ وَالسَّلَامُ	May Allāh send Blessings & Safety upon him (i.e. a Prophet or Messenger)
صَلَّى اللهُ عَلَيْهِ وَعَلَى آلِهِ وَسَلَّمَ	May Allāh send Blessings & Safety upon him and his family (i.e. Du'ā sent when mentioning the Prophet Muhammad)
رَحْمَةُ اللهِ	May Allāh have mercy upon him
رَضِيَ اللهُ عَنْهُمْ	May Allāh be pleased with them (i.e. Du'ā made for the Companions of the Prophet Muhammad)
جَلَّ جَلَالُهُ	(Allāh) His Majesty is Exalted
رَضِيَ اللهُ عَنْهَا	رَضِيَ اللهُ عَنْهَا (i.e. a female companion of the Prophet Muhammad)

TEN PREVENTIVE MEASURES AGAINST MAGIC AND ENVY

مُقَدِّمَة

INTRODUCTION

All praise is due to Allāh. We thank Him, seek His assistance, seek His forgiveness, and repent to Him. We seek refuge in Allāh from the evil of ourselves and our wicked actions. Certainly, whoever Allāh guides, none shall lead him astray; and whomever is misled, none can guide him. I bear witness that there is none worthy of worship, but Allāh with no partner and that Muhammad is His servant and Messenger; may Allāh's peace and blessings be upon him, his family and his companions. O Allāh, the knowledge we have is what you allowed us to know. O Allāh lead us to what benefits us and increase us in knowledge, and

INTRODUCTION

make the knowledge we learn on our favor not against us. We invoke for your guidance and assistance in doing all that is good, and to never let us handle our own selves for the blink of an eye.

Our discussion is about the ten preventive measures one should employ and maintain if afflicted with magic or envy, in order to rid oneself of them by Allāh's permission. A true believer always resorts and turns to Allāh (سُبْحَانَهُوَتَعَالَى) in everything in his life. For certainly, Allāh is the only One from whom one can seek assistance, success, and well-being. Such believer asks none but Allāh for all of his needs, on Whose Hand lies the control of everything.

Any human being is vulnerable to be tested with some kind of envy or magic, or whatever else from this sort of thing, whose (existence) and true effect on the human being have been confirmed by the textual evidence. It may take the form of a sickness, an ailment,

TEN PREVENTIVE MEASURES AGAINST MAGIC AND ENVY

or any kind of other distresses. And upon the occurrence of such thing, people take different healing measures in order to gain their health back and steer clear of them.

Notably, if a person suffers from a desperate shortage in knowledge of the implications of the textual evidence of Qur'ān and Sunnah in addition to the company of a bad instructor, such person will certainly be the victim of superstitions and the unlimited means of misguidance. A lot of people fall for superstitions, which have notorious circulation among them, due to lack of knowledge and insight of the religion of Allāh.

Superstitions, as a matter of fact, grow rampantly in an atmosphere of increasing ignorance, sins, and ailments; the more such things increase, the more rampant superstition become. In contrast, once sound knowledge, which is based on Qur'ān and Sunnah,

INTRODUCTION

exists, an atmosphere of welfare, uprightness, and virtue is bound to prevail; and eventually, people's affairs in this life and in the one to come shall be in the best of shape.

To follow up, one of Allāh's graces upon the believer at a time where he is afflicted with sickness or hardship is that he turns to none but Allāh (سُبْحَانَهُ وَتَعَالَى); as He says:

$$\text{﴿ فَفِرُّوٓا۟ إِلَى ٱللَّهِ ﴾}$$

"So flee to Allāh." [Sūrah Adh-Dhariyat 51:50]

And as the Prophet (صَلَّى ٱللَّهُ عَلَيْهِ وَسَلَّمَ) said,

$$\text{لَا مَلْجَأَ وَ لَا مَنْجَا مِنْكَ إِلَّا إِلَيْكَ}$$

"There is no resort nor salvation from You except to You."

TEN PREVENTIVE MEASURES AGAINST MAGIC AND ENVY

Resort is surely to Allāh alone. He is more than satisfactory for whoever trusts in Him. He grants assistance for whoever seeks it, and refuge for whoever asks for it. People, in this contemporary time, are in absolute need for guided instructions in the light of the textual evidence from Qur'ān and the Sunnah of His Prophet (ﷺ), whenever an occasion of affliction of such sort arises.

Ibn al-Qayyim (رحمه الله) addressed this issue in a quite thorough and elaborate manner in his book *'Bada' al-Fawā'id'* when he was interpreting the meanings of Allāh's saying:

﴿ قُلْ أَعُوذُ بِرَبِّ ٱلْفَلَقِ ۝ مِن شَرِّ مَا خَلَقَ ۝ وَمِن شَرِّ غَاسِقٍ إِذَا وَقَبَ ۝ وَمِن شَرِّ ٱلنَّفَّٰثَٰتِ فِي ٱلْعُقَدِ ۝ وَمِن شَرِّ حَاسِدٍ إِذَا حَسَدَ ۝ ﴾

INTRODUCTION

> "Say: I seek refuge with (Allāh) the Lord of the daybreak. From the evil of what He has created; And from the evil of the darkening (night) as it comes with its darkness; (or the moon as it sets or goes away). And from the evil of the witchcrafts when they blow in the knots, and from the evil of the envier when he envies."
>
> [*Sūrah al-Falaq* 113:1-5]

During his interpretation of the meanings of this great Surah, he explored envy and magic; and then he elaborated quite superbly the preventive measures that should be employed by whoever is afflicted with such distress to rid himself eventually of it. He mentioned ten preventive measures any victim of such distress (magic or envy) must embrace. I remember once, an African brother approached me relating to me that his son was afflicted with such distress six months ago. His son is now lying in bed since then, and he is

TEN PREVENTIVE MEASURES AGAINST MAGIC AND ENVY

still young. I referred him to read the words of al-'Alaamah ibn al-Qayyim. I advised him to study carefully and absorb his words, and then he should call his son, translate, explain, and instruct him to practice those words; and he shall see promising results by Allāh's permission. Few days later, he called me relaying to me the good news that his son called him to let him know that everything is fine, and he no longer feels a thing.

There are similar situations, and it's all in Allāh's hands. Allāh must always be the person's first and final resort, which is an expression of one's true servitude to Allāh. The person, in this life, is indeed a servant to Allāh; every single aspect of one's life should reflect this fact. Gratitude at a time of receiving a blessing and patience at times of ordeals are an expression of this servitude. One, therefore, should

INTRODUCTION

embrace the different expressions of servitude required by each life situation one lives. Such expressions include trust in Allāh, reliance, obedience, supplication, humility, and hope in Allāh among many other expressions, which considered to be the Muslim's attitude and habit.

The Ten preventive measures are:

TEN PREVENTIVE MEASURES AGAINST MAGIC AND ENVY

THE FIRST MEASURE: TO SEEK REFUGE IN ALLĀH

To seek refuge in Allāh (سُبْحَانَهُوَتَعَالَى) from the evil of such distress (i.e. envy and magic). Also, to resort to Allāh and seek His protection.

Allāh says,

﴿ قُلْ أَعُوذُ بِرَبِّ ٱلْفَلَقِ ۝ مِن شَرِّ مَا خَلَقَ ۝ وَمِن شَرِّ غَاسِقٍ إِذَا وَقَبَ ۝ وَمِن شَرِّ ٱلنَّفَّٰثَٰتِ فِى ٱلْعُقَدِ ۝ وَمِن شَرِّ حَاسِدٍ إِذَا حَسَدَ ۝ ﴾

THE FIRST MEASURE: TO SEEK REFUGE IN ALLĀH

"Say: I seek refuge with (Allāh) the Lord of the daybreak. From the evil of what He has created; And from the evil of the darkening (night) as it comes with its darkness; (or the moon as it sets or goes away). And from the evil of the witchcrafts when they blow in the knots, referring to the magicians. And from the evil of the envier when he envies." [*Sūrah al-Falaq* 113:1-5]

Allāh (سُبْحَانَهُوَتَعَالَى) certainly hears and knows whoever sought refuge in Him, and He is capable of everything. He alone is to be sought for help. None merits this right but Him because He is the One, who provides help and protection against whatever the cause for refuge. The genuine essence of refuge is resorting to Allāh and seeking His protection. Simply, it is to flee away from a fearful thing and resort to whoever provides protection against it. And Allāh,

TEN PREVENTIVE MEASURES AGAINST MAGIC AND ENVY

alone, is the One to whom one resorts, seeks refuge and protection. Actually, the very act of refuge is an act of servitude that must be devoted to Allāh solely. Accordingly, one must immediately resort to Allāh once an ordeal befalls him.

﴿ وَإِمَّا يَنزَغَنَّكَ مِنَ ٱلشَّيْطَٰنِ نَزْغٌ فَٱسْتَعِذْ بِٱللَّهِ إِنَّهُۥ سَمِيعٌ عَلِيمٌ ۝ ﴾

"Should a temptation from Satan disturb *you*, invoke the protection of Allāh; indeed, He is all-hearing, all-knowing." [Sūrah al-A'rāf 7:200]

﴿ وَمَن يَعْتَصِم بِٱللَّهِ فَقَدْ هُدِىَ إِلَىٰ صِرَٰطٍ مُّسْتَقِيمٍ ﴾

THE FIRST MEASURE: TO SEEK REFUGE IN ALLĀH

"And whoever takes recourse in Allāh is certainly guided to a straight path." [Sūrah Aali Imrān 3:101]

$$﴿ وَقُل رَّبِّ أَعُوذُ بِكَ مِنْ هَمَزَاتِ ٱلشَّيَاطِينِ ۝ وَأَعُوذُ بِكَ رَبِّ أَن يَحْضُرُونِ ۝ ﴾$$

"And say, 'My Lord! I seek Your protection from the promptings of devils; and I seek Your protection, my Lord, from their presence near me." [Sūrah al-Mu'minoon 23:97-98]

Allāh never lets anybody down whenever one is sincere in seeking refuge, resort, and protection. He rather backs such person with His assistance, protection, and success.

THE SECOND MEASURE: TO HAVE TAQWĀ

To have Taqwā. One should commit to Taqwā in (literally) everything in one's life. Never has it ever been just a claim, but rather an actual implementation of its essence. Its essence is to observe Allāh's obligation and abandon His prohibitions. For this particular essence, Talq ibn Habib (رَحِمَهُٱللَّهُ) defined Taqwā when asked about it,

THE SECOND MEASURE: TO HAVE TAQWĀ

$$\text{أَنْ تَعْمَلَ بِطَاعَةِ اللهِ عَلَى نُورٍ مِنَ اللهِ تَرْجُو ثَوَابَ اللهِ، وَ أَنْ تَتْرُكَ مَعْصِيَةَ اللهِ عَلَى نُورٍ مِنَ اللهِ تَخَافُ عِقَابَ اللهِ.}$$

"it is to obey Allāh in the manner He prescribed out of hoping for His reward. Likewise, to abandon disobeying Allāh in the manner, He prescribed out of fear of His punishment."

One should familiarize oneself with the commands of Allāh in order to observe them as well as His prohibitions to avoid them. So, ultimately, one would be able to achieve Taqwā. Allāh says,

$$\text{﴿وَالْعَاقِبَةُ لِلْمُتَّقِينَ ۝﴾}$$

"Verily, the good end awaits the *Muttaqūn* (obedient, righteous)." [*Sūrah al-A'rāf* 7:128]

TEN PREVENTIVE MEASURES AGAINST MAGIC AND ENVY

People who observe Taqwā have retained the most pleasant end in addition to rest, tranquility, and safety in this life and the hereafter.

﴿ وَمَن يَتَّقِ ٱللَّهَ يَجْعَل لَّهُ مَخْرَجًا ۝ وَيَرْزُقْهُ مِنْ حَيْثُ لَا يَحْتَسِبُ وَمَن يَتَوَكَّلْ عَلَى ٱللَّهِ فَهُوَ حَسْبُهُۥٓ ﴾

"And whoever has Taqwā of Allāh, He shall make a way out for him 'and provide for him from whence he does not reckon." [Sūrah at-Talaq 65:2-3]

﴿ وَمَن يَتَّقِ ٱللَّهَ يَجْعَل لَّهُ مِنْ أَمْرِهِۦ يُسْرًا ﴾

"And whoever has Taqwā of Allāh, He shall grant him ease in his affairs." [Sūrah at-Talaq 65:4]

THE SECOND MEASURE: TO HAVE TAQWĀ

Notably, easiness, pleasant end, success, and blessings are all fruits of Taqwa. Those fruits are countless, and they are reserved for the committed obedient. So whoever embraces Taqwa shall be protected by Allāh, Who will never fail him. One can notice such fact in Allāh's saying:

﴿ وَإِن تَصْبِرُوا۟ وَتَتَّقُوا۟ لَا يَضُرُّكُمْ كَيْدُهُمْ شَيْئًا ﴾

"Yet if you are patient and God-wary, their guile will not harm you in any way." [*Sūrah Ali Imran* 3:120]

It means that no matter how deceptive they could ever be, their deception is simply useless; why? Because a person who is a committed obedient is under Allāh's protection; so who could possibly harm a person Allāh protects?!

The Prophet (ﷺ) said,

TEN PREVENTIVE MEASURES AGAINST MAGIC AND ENVY

احْفَظِ اللهَ يَحْفَظْكَ، احْفَظِ اللهَ تَجِدْهُ تُجَاهَكَ

"Be ever mindful of Allāh, and He shall protect you; be ever-mindful of Allāh and you shall find Him whenever you need Him."

To be mindful of Allāh is by observing His obligations and staying away from His prohibitions. In return, Allāh shall bless your health, money, and every aspect of one's life. So whoever is ever-mindful of Allāh, Allāh shall always provide him with success and assistance; not to mention, since Allāh on his side, from whom could he be afraid of?

It is noteworthy to state that fear of human beings is the result of weakness of faith and Taqwā. Scholars have stressed particularly on the issue that weakness of faith in the heart produces fear; whereas strong Tawhīd (Monotheism), faith, and Taqwā in the heart of

THE SECOND MEASURE: TO HAVE TAQWĀ

the Muslim leaves no space for fear except from Allāh and singles out resort to anybody but Him. In short, Taqwā is a critical and necessary requirement for ridding of evil and for asking for blessings in this life and the hereafter.

Acquiring Taqwā along with faith bring good and blessings in one's wealth, family, life, provision, health, and all aspects of life.

TEN PREVENTIVE MEASURES AGAINST MAGIC AND ENVY

THE THIRD MEASURE: ENDURING THE HARM OF ONE'S ENEMY

Enduring the harm of one's enemy. The word enemy, in this context, includes anyone who envies you or casted a magical spell against you. One should endure such enemy, and neither engage aggressively with him in any encounter, nor complain to people about him, nor even entertain the idea of harming him. The truth is the only way to defeat one's enemy is by enduring his harm; because the more transgression the envier gets but faced by endurance from the transgressed, the more strength and power the transgressed will accumulate against his enemy without the latter feeling it.

This point is very crucial if properly understood. It (redefines) transgression as an arrow thrown by the transgressor against himself. The proof is:

﴿ وَلَا يَحِيقُ ٱلْمَكْرُ ٱلسَّيِّئُ إِلَّا بِأَهْلِهِۦ ﴾

"**And evil schemes beset only their authors.**" [*Sūrah Fāṭir* 35:43]

Achieving this will help one to go on with his life, work, worship, and not only endure the harm of his enemy but also dispel any concerns about it; also, being free to capitalize on his interests in both this life and the hereafter. Ibn al-Qayyim remarked,

TEN PREVENTIVE MEASURES AGAINST MAGIC AND ENVY

مَا انْتَصَرَ إِنْسَانٌ عَلَى حَاسِدِهِ وَ عَدُوِّهِ بِمِثْلِ هَذَا الْمَقَامِ الْعَظِيمِ مَقَامِ الصَّبْرِ، فَإِذَا صَبَرَ الْمَحْسُودُ وَ لَمْ يَسْتَطِلَّ الْأَمْرَ نَالَ حُسْنَ الْعَاقِبَةِ بِإِذْنِ اللهِ تَبَارَكَ وَ تَعَالَى فَمَا نَصَرَ عَلَى حَاسِدِهِ وَ عَدُوِّهِ بِمِثْلِ الصَّبْرِ عَلَيْهِ وَ التَّوَكُّلِ عَلَى اللهِ وَ لَا يَسْتَطِلُّ تَأْخِيرُهُ وَ بَغْيِهِ فَإِنَّهُ كُلَّمَا بَغَى عَلَيْهِ كَانَ بَغْيُهُ جُنْدًا وَ قُوَّةً لِلْمَبْغِي عَلَيْهِ الْمَحْسُودُ يُقَاتِلُ بِهِ الْبَاغِي نَفْسَهُ وَ هُوَ لَا يُشْعَرُ. فَبَغْيَهُ سِهَامٌ يَرْمِيهَا مِنْ نَفْسِهِ وَ لَوْ رَأَى الْمَبْغِي عَلَيْهِ ذَلِكَ لَسَرَّهُ بَغْيَةَ

"Nothing but endurance is the tool for one's triumph over his enemy. If endurance were to be employed, pleasant consequences are awaiting by Allāh's permission. One can win over his envier through endurance and trust in Allāh; because the more transgression the envier gets if faced by endurance from the transgressed, the more strength and power the transgressed will accumulate against his enemy without the latter feeling it. In brief, transgression is a self-inflicting damage. However, if the transgressed were to understand this fact, he would be pleased for such transgression."

TEN PREVENTIVE MEASURES AGAINST MAGIC AND ENVY

THE FOURTH MEASURE:

TRUST IN ALLĀH

Trust in Allāh. It is to have full confidence and reliance on Allāh accompanied by seeking the means authorized in Allāh's Book and the Sunnah of His Prophet (ﷺ). Trust in Allāh is one of the most efficient means to fend off any unbearable harm, oppression, or enmity.

Allāh says,

﴿ أَلَيْسَ ٱللَّهُ بِكَافٍ عَبْدَهُۥ ﴾

THE FOURTH MEASURE: TRUST IN ALLĀH

"Is not Allāh Sufficient for His slave?" [*Sūrah az-Zumar* 39:36]

Allāh says,

$$\text{﴿ وَمَن يَتَوَكَّلْ عَلَى ٱللَّهِ فَهُوَ حَسْبُهُۥٓ ﴾}$$

"**And whosoever puts his trust in Allāh, then He will suffice him.**" [*Sūrah at-Talaaq* 65:3]

Based on this, whomever is sufficed by Allāh, he is no longer a target for any enemy. To the point even if all those on this earth or the heavens conspired against him, Allāh would protect him and secure a way out for him if he were to fully and truly trusts in Allāh. This matter is illustrated on various hadiths. For instance, the Prophet's saying to Ibn 'Abbas,

TEN PREVENTIVE MEASURES AGAINST MAGIC AND ENVY

وَاعْلَمْ أَنَّ الْأُمَّةَ لَوْ اجْتَمَعَتْ عَلَى أَنْ يَنْفَعُوكَ بِشَيْءٍ لَمْ يَنْفَعُوكَ إِلَّا بِشَيْءٍ قَدْ كَتَبَهُ اللهُ لَكَ، وَلَوْ اجْتَمَعُوا عَلَى أَنْ يَضُرُّوكَ بِشَيْءٍ لَمْ يَضُرُّوكَ إِلَّا بِشَيْءٍ قَدْ كَتَبَهُ اللهُ عَلَيْكَ، رُفِعَتِ الْأَقْلَامُ وَجَفَّتِ الصُّحُفُ.

"And know that if the nation were to gather together to benefit you with anything, they would not benefit you except with what Allāh had already prescribed for you. And if they were to gather together to harm you with anything, they would not harm you except with what Allāh had already prescribed against you. The pens have been lifted, and the pages have dried."

THE FOURTH MEASURE: TRUST IN ALLĀH

When Musa and his followers fled from Egypt to rescue their faith. Pharaoh chased them with countless numbers of soldiers and powerful ordinance material. When Musa reached the sea along with his followers, they looked back and witnessed a huge military force led by Pharaoh; the kind of force they were unable to stand against. Musa's followers complained to him.

﴿ إِنَّا لَمُدْرَكُونَ ۝ ﴾

"We will be caught." [Sūrah ash-Shu'arā 26:61]

The sea is right in front of us while Pharaoh and his force are behind us, and there is no way out. In other words, our death is certain as we are trapped between the sea and Pharaoh. Musa voiced out confidently with full trust in Allāh,

TEN PREVENTIVE MEASURES AGAINST MAGIC AND ENVY

$$﴿ كَلَّا إِنَّ مَعِيَ رَبِّي سَيَهْدِينِ ۝ ﴾$$

"Nay, verily! With me is my Lord, He will guide me." [Sūrah ash-Shu'arā 26: 62]

Allāh instructed him to,

$$﴿ أَضْرِب بِّعَصَاكَ ٱلْبَحْرَ ﴾$$

"Strike the sea with your stick,"

Which he did. Then,

$$﴿ فَٱنفَلَقَ فَكَانَ كُلُّ فِرْقٍ كَٱلطَّوْدِ ٱلْعَظِيمِ ۝ ﴾$$

"And it parted, and each separate part (of that sea water) became like the huge, firm mass of a mountain." [Sūrah ash-Shu'arā 26:63]

THE FOURTH MEASURE: TRUST IN ALLĀH

And it parted, and each separate part (of that sea water) became like the huge, firm mass of a mountain. The seabed has become waterless and dry floor without any mud or stickiness. Musa tread this floor along with his followers all the way to the other end. The Pharaoh had reached the opposite end, and he decided to go after Musa and his followers.

By the time Musa and his followers were all out of the sea, Allāh ordered the water to go back to its original form at the very time Pharaoh, and his entire military force were in the sea. Every last one of them including Pharaoh, who used to say arrogantly,

هَـذِهِ الْأَنْـهَـارُ تَـجْـرِي مِـنْ تَـحْـتِـي ، أَنَـا رَبُّ الْـعَـالَـمِـيـنَ

"these rivers flowing underneath me," and, "I'm the Lord of the worlds,"

TEN PREVENTIVE MEASURES AGAINST MAGIC AND ENVY

ended up drowning, despite the useless faith he announced,

﴿ءَامَنتُ أَنَّهُ لَآ إِلَٰهَ إِلَّا ٱلَّذِىٓ ءَامَنَتْ بِهِۦ بَنُوٓا۟ إِسْرَٰٓءِيلَ﴾ ﴿٩٠﴾

"I believe that La ilaha illa (Huwa): (none has the right to be worshiped but) He," in Whom the Children of Israel believe." [Sūrah Yunus 10:90]

The bottom line is that trust in Allāh secures one's salvation no matter the circumstances.

Jabir bin `Abdullah narrated that he proceeded in the company of Allāh's Messenger (ﷺ) towards Najd to participate in a Ghazwa (military expedition). When Allāh's Messenger (ﷺ) returned, he too

THE FOURTH MEASURE: TRUST IN ALLĀH

returned with him. Midday came upon them while they were in a valley having many thorny trees. Allāh's Messenger (ﷺ) and the people dismounted and dispersed to rest in the shade of the trees. Allāh's Messenger (ﷺ) rested under a tree and hung his sword on it. We all took a nap and suddenly we heard Allāh's Messenger (ﷺ) calling us. "(We woke up) to see a Bedouin with him. The Prophet (ﷺ) said,

إِنَّ هَذَا اخْتَرَطَ عَلَيَّ سَيْفِي وَ أَنَا نَائِمٌ

فَاسْتَيْقَظْتُ وَ هُوَ فِي يَدِهِ صَلْتًا فَقَالَ: مَنْ

يَمْنَعُكَ مِنِّي فَقُلْتُ اللهُ ثَلَاثًا وَ لَمْ يُعَاقِبْهُ وَ

جَلَسَ.

TEN PREVENTIVE MEASURES AGAINST MAGIC AND ENVY

"This Bedouin took out my sword while I was sleeping and when I woke up, I found the unsheathed sword in his hand, and he challenged me saying, 'Who will save you from me?' I said thrice, 'Allāh.' The Prophet (ﷺ) did not punish him but sat down. So, he put the sword back into its scabbard, and you see him sitting here." Anyhow, the Prophet (ﷺ) did not punish him." [Recorded by al-Bukhārī]

Imam Ahmad related,

قَاتَلَ رَسُولُ اللهِ صَلَّى اللهُ عَلَيْهِ وَ سَلَّمَ مُحَارِبَ

خَصَفَةَ بِنَخْلٍ فَرَأَوْا مِنَ الْمُسْلِمِينَ غِرَّةً فَجَاءَ

رَجُلٌ مِنْهُمْ يُقَالُ لَهُ غَوْرَتُ بْنُ الْحَارِثِ حَتَّى قَامَ

عَلَى رَأْسِ رَسُولِ اللهِ (صَلَّى اللهُ عَلَيْهِ وَ سَلَّمَ)

THE FOURTH MEASURE: TRUST IN ALLĀH

بِالسَّيْفِ فَقَالَ مَنْ يَمْنَعُكَ مِنِّي قَالَ اللهُ عَزَّ وَ جَلَّ فَسَقَطَ السَّيْفُ مِنْ يَدِهِ فَأَخَذَهُ رَسُولُ اللهِ صَلَّى اللهُ عَلَيْهِ وَ سَلَّمَ فَقَالَ مَنْ يَمْنَعُكَ مِنِّي قَالَ: كُنْ كَخَيْرِ آخِذٍ.

"The Messenger of Allāh (ﷺ) fought a tribe called (Muhārib Khasafah). The disbelievers took Muslims by surprise until one of them named Ghaurath bin al-Hārith approached the Messenger of Allāh (ﷺ) very close near his head holding the sword. He challenged the prophet, "Who will save you from me?" The Prophet replied, "Allāh (سُبْحَانَهُ وَتَعَالَى)." The sword fell from his hand; the Prophet picked it up and said, "Who will save

TEN PREVENTIVE MEASURES AGAINST MAGIC AND ENVY

you from me now?" He begged the Prophet, "Be better than me."

Based on this whenever one relies on Allāh (سُبْحَانَهُ وَتَعَالَى) he is sufficed by Allāh to the point even if all on this earth or in the heavens conspired against him. Because all of the matters are in Allāh's Hands; so whatever He wills comes into existence and whatever He doesn't will not exist, and we have no might and power through Allāh.

THE FIFTH MEASURE: TO EMPTY THE HEART FROM THINKING

To empty the heart from thinking about it. One should clear his heart from any thoughts related to the envier. A lot of people sustain health problems because they think long and hard about their envier; sometimes it may be just an illusion. They worry too much until they get sick. At any rate, one of the critical measures is to empty your mind of thinking about it. Also, one should dismiss this very thought once it crosses the mind. Ibn al-Qayyim notes,

TEN PREVENTIVE MEASURES AGAINST MAGIC AND ENVY

$$\text{وَ هَـذَا مِـنْ أَنْـفَـعُ الْأَدْوِيَـةِ وَ أَقْـوَى الْأَسْبَـابِ الْـمُـعِـيـنَـةِ}$$

$$\text{عَـلَى انْدِفَـاعِ شَـرِّهِ.}$$

"This is one of the most healing measures to fend off the danger of such evil (referring to envy and magic)."

He provided an illustrative example, "keep thinking about the envier is the same as offering oneself voluntarily for the enemy."

Consider this: someone is walking on the street, where there are some wicked and abusive people. They abused him verbally; in this situation, if he were to react to their abuse and decide to engage, what would happen? It will definitely get worse given their wickedness and disregard for inflicting unlimited harm. The longer he engages in dispute with them, the more time he wastes, with absolutely no avail but only

THE FIFTH MEASURE: TO EMPTY THE HEART FROM THINKING

more harm and damage. On the contrary, it is strongly advisable to avoid them and be completely disregardful of their presence. Just like in Allāh's saying:

$$﴿ وَأَعْرِضْ عَنِ ٱلْجَٰهِلِينَ ۝ ﴾$$

"Turn away from the foolish (i.e. don't punish them)." [Sūrah al-'A'rāf 7:199]

Similarly, a poet beautifully composed:

$$وَ لَقَدْ أَمُرُّ عَلَى السَّفِيهِ يَسُبُّنِي$$

$$فَأَمُرُّ ثَمَّةَ وَ أَقُولُ لَا يَعْنِينِي$$

"I may, by chance, pass by a foolish who insults me,

I would ignore him believing he does not mean me."

TEN PREVENTIVE MEASURES AGAINST MAGIC AND ENVY

The reason is: if he were to stop, turn to him and argue with him, he would trouble himself, sustain mental and bodily damage, and end up with nothing at all. This very point is highlighted by Ibn al-Qayyim by drawing an example,

> "it is as if one's enemy deliberately provokes hostility against him. If the person avoids such provocative advance and disengages, the enemy will certainly fail; but if he is provoked and engaged, the damage is bound to happen."

He continues,

> "If both were to engage in dispute, peace would have no place and nothing but evil is the replacement until one of them collapses. Conversely, if the person maintains composure and restraint from busying the mind with overthinking about it (i.e. envy), in addition to dismissing the very thought of it once it crosses the mind and busying oneself with what's more

THE FIFTH MEASURE: TO EMPTY THE HEART FROM THINKING

beneficial instead, his envier will be eating his heart out. Because envy is like fire, and unless there is nothing to consume, it will consume itself."

TEN PREVENTIVE MEASURES AGAINST MAGIC AND ENVY

THE SIXTH MEASURE: DEVOTION AND SINCERITY TO ALLĀH

Devotion and sincerity to Allāh. One should let the love, repent, and the request for the pleasure of Allāh slip into the heart until they are powerful enough to overwhelm (the negative) thoughts and neutralize them completely. In other words, the one who is tested with such ordeal (i.e. magic or envy) should seek healing by enlivening his heart with sincerity, love, devotion, and faith in Allāh. One should keep this up until it fills the whole heart and leaves no place for anything else.

THE SIXTH MEASURE: DEVOTION AND SINCERITY TO ALLĀH

Following this measure ought to make all the person's thoughts, premonitions, and hope fixed on seeking to please, invoke, beseech, and remember Allāh. Allāh related in the Qur'ān that His enemy, Iblīs, said:

$$\text{فَبِعِزَّتِكَ لَأُغْوِيَنَّهُمْ أَجْمَعِينَ ۝ إِلَّا عِبَادَكَ مِنْهُمُ الْمُخْلَصِينَ ۝}$$

"By Your Might, then I will surely mislead them all, except Your chosen slaves amongst them (faithful, obedient, true believers of Islamic Monotheism)." [Sūrah Sa'ad 38:82-83]

The devil is absolutely powerless in the face of the sincere. The sincere is like a person who sought shelter in an invincible fort that keeps everybody safe, secure, and considered by the enemy to be a lost cause. The happiness of those inside this fort is incomparable.

TEN PREVENTIVE MEASURES AGAINST MAGIC AND ENVY

This measure is of critical need in order to heal from this matter in question and any other; since sincerity is the mean for every good, happiness, and success in this life and the hereafter.

THE SEVENTH MEASURE: TO FILTER OUT ONE'S REPENTANCE TO ALLĀH FROM ALL SINS

To filter out one's repentance to Allāh from all sins that were the primary cause for having enemies. Allāh says:

﴿ وَمَآ أَصَـٰبَكُم مِّن مُّصِيبَةٍ فَبِمَا كَسَبَتْ أَيْدِيكُمْ وَيَعْفُواْ عَن كَثِيرٍ ۝ ﴾

"And whatever of misfortune befalls you, it is because of what your hands have earned."
[Sūrah ash-Shūrā 42:30]

TEN PREVENTIVE MEASURES AGAINST MAGIC AND ENVY

Any enemy including enviers is the result of one's sins. Logically, one of the most effective means of treatment is sincere repentance to Allāh. Allāh says:

﴿ يَٰٓأَيُّهَا ٱلَّذِينَ ءَامَنُواْ تُوبُوٓاْ إِلَى ٱللَّهِ تَوۡبَةٗ نَّصُوحٗا ﴾

"O you who believe! Turn to Allāh with sincere repentance!" [Sūrah at-Tahrīm 66:8]

The scholars have remarked that true repentance requires three conditions: to regret the sin, to abandon it, and to resolve never commit it again. But if the sin involves wronging another human being, asking for forgiveness or giving his right back is to be added to the previous conditions. Ibn al-Qayyim noted,

فَمَا سُلِّطَ عَلَى الْعَبْدِ مَنْ يُؤْذِيهِ إِلَّا بِذَنْبٍ

يَعْلَمُهُ أَوْ لَا يَعْلَمُهُ، وَ مَا لَا يَعْلَمُهُ الْعَبْدُ مِنْ

THE SEVENTH MEASURE: TO FILTER OUT ONE'S REPENTANCE TO ALLĀH FROM ALL SINS

ذُنُوبِهِ أَضْعَافَ مَا يَعْلَمُهُ مِنْهَا، وَ مَا يَنْسَاهُ مِمَّا عَلِمَهُ وَ عَمِلَهُ أَضْعَافَ مَا يَذْكُرُهُ.

"Harm is brought upon a person because of the sins one committed whether one knows them or not. Actually, not only the number of sins one does not know is multiple times more than what one knows but also the ones he forgot after prior knowledge of them are multiple times more than those he didn't forget."

Hence, one should repent from every single sin he committed whether he knows them or otherwise. Ibn al-Qayyim urged,

TEN PREVENTIVE MEASURES AGAINST MAGIC AND ENVY

فَمَا يَحْتَاجُ الْعَبْدُ إِلَى الِاسْتِغْفَارِ مِنْهُ مِمَّا لَا يَعْلَمُهُ - أَيْ مِنْ ذُنُوبِ نَفْسِهِ - أَضْعَافَ أَضْعَافَ مِمَّا يَعْلَمُهُ، فَمَا سُلِّطَ عَلَيْهِ مُؤْذٍ إِلَّا بِذَنْبٍ ... لَيْسَ فِي الْوُجُودِ شَرٌّ إِلَّا الذُّنُوبُ وَ مُوجِبَاتُهَا، فَإِذَا عُوفِيَ مِنَ الذُّنُوبِ عُوفِيَ مِنْ مُوجِبَاتِهَا، فَلَيْسَ لِلْعَبْدِ إِذَا بُغِيَ عَلَيْهِ وَ أُوذِيَ وَ تَسَلَّطُ عَلَيْهِ خُصُومُهُ شَيْءٌ أَنْفَعُ لَهُ مِنَ التَّوْبَةِ النَّصُوحِ

"one should seek forgiveness from the sins he does not know, as they are multiple times more than what he knows. Sin is the cause behind any harm inflicted on the human being, as there is nothing more dangerous in this existence

53 | Page

THE SEVENTH MEASURE: TO FILTER OUT ONE'S REPENTANCE TO ALLĀH FROM ALL SINS

> than sins and their consequences. Once sins are removed, their consequences will be gone as well. In short, nothing but sincere repentance is the repellent of any harm brought about by one's enemies."

In a regard, the very existence of an enemy may be enough a cause for the person to repent to Allāh, and in this case, it would be like a wake-up call. Many people spend a long time oblivious of their religion, but when their enemy troubles them, they realize that this is due to their sins. In this case, the existence of the enemy was their ticket to repent to Allāh; indeed, this is a blessing and success for the believer.

TEN PREVENTIVE MEASURES AGAINST MAGIC AND ENVY

THE EIGHTH MEASURE: TO GIVE OUT CHARITY

To give out charity as much as possible. The Prophet says,

الصَّدَقَةُ تُطْفِيءُ غَضَبَ الرَّبِّ

"**Charity makes the anger of Allāh fade away.**"

And he also said,

دَاوُوا مَرْضَاكُمْ بِالصَّدَقَةِ

"**Cure your sick with charity.**".

This proves the great benefit of charity.

Ibn al-Qayyim said,

THE EIGHTH MEASURE: TO GIVE OUT CHARITY

فَإِنَّ لِذَلِكَ تَأْثِيراً عَجِيباً فِي دَفْعِ الْبَلَاءِ وَ دَفْعِ الْعَيْنِ وَ شَرِّ الْحَاسِدِ ... فَمَا يَكَادُ الْعَيْنُ وَ الْحَسَدُ وَ الْأَذَى يَتَسَلَّطُ عَلَى مُحْسِنٍ مُتَصَدِّقٍ، وَ إِنْ أَصَابَهُ شَيْءٌ مِنْ ذَلِكَ كَانَ مُعَامَلاً فِيهِ بِاللُّطْفِ وَ الْمَعُونَةِ وَ التَّأْيِيدِ، وَ كَانَتْ لَهُ فِيهِ الْعَافِيَةُ وَ الْعَاقِبَةُ الْحَمِيدَةُ - وَ الصَّدَقَةُ وَ الْإِحْسَانُ مِنْ شُكْرِ النِّعْمَةِ - ... فَالشُّكْرُ حَارِسُ النِّعْمَةِ مِنْ كُلِّ مَا يَكُونُ سَبَباً لِزَوَالِهَا.

"Charity has a very wondrous impact on repelling ordeals and fending off envy. It is almost as if it keeps its payer impenetrable;

TEN PREVENTIVE MEASURES AGAINST MAGIC AND ENVY

even if such person is inflicted to some extent with such ordeal, he is supported, and the harm is lessened; not to mention regaining wellness and a good end. Charity is actually an expression of gratitude for Allāh's blessings. And gratitude is the guardian for Allāh's graces against anything that could be the reason for taking them away."

The scholars describe **'gratitude'** as either **'the preserver'** or **'the importer'**; because it preserves the existing graces of Allāh and imports the lost ones.

﴿ وَإِذْ تَأَذَّنَ رَبُّكُمْ لَئِن شَكَرْتُمْ لَأَزِيدَنَّكُمْ وَلَئِن كَفَرْتُمْ إِنَّ عَذَابِي لَشَدِيدٌ ۝ ﴾

"And (remember) when your Lord proclaimed: "If you give thanks (by accepting Faith and

THE EIGHTH MEASURE: TO GIVE OUT CHARITY

worshipping none but Allāh), I will give you more (of My Blessings), but if you are thankless (i.e. disbelievers), verily! My Punishment is indeed severe." [*Sūrah Ibrāhīm* 14:7]

TEN PREVENTIVE MEASURES AGAINST MAGIC AND ENVY

THE NINTH MEASURE: TO SUPPRESS THE BLAZING FURY OF THE ENVIER

To suppress the blazing fury of the envier and the transgressor by acting gently and friendly with him. You should be even more friendly, advising, and sympathetic when his envy, transgression, and envy increases; but, who has it in him? Read carefully Allāh's saying:

THE NINTH MEASURE: TO SUPPRESS THE BLAZING FURY OF THE ENVIER

﴿ وَلَا تَسْتَوِي ٱلْحَسَنَةُ وَلَا ٱلسَّيِّئَةُ ٱدْفَعْ بِٱلَّتِي هِيَ أَحْسَنُ فَإِذَا ٱلَّذِي بَيْنَكَ وَبَيْنَهُ عَدَاوَةٌ كَأَنَّهُ وَلِيٌّ حَمِيمٌ ﴾

"The good deed and the evil deed cannot be equal. Repel (the evil) with one that is better (i.e. Allāh ordered the faithful believers to be patient at the time of anger, and to excuse those who treat them badly), then verily! He, between whom and you there was enmity, (will become) as though he was a close friend." [Sūrah Fussilāt 41:34]

But who has enough patience to endure this?! Allāh says:

TEN PREVENTIVE MEASURES AGAINST MAGIC AND ENVY

﴿ وَمَا يُلَقَّىٰهَا إِلَّا ٱلَّذِينَ صَبَرُوا۟ وَمَا يُلَقَّىٰهَا إِلَّا ذُو حَظٍّ عَظِيمٍ ﴾

"But none is granted it (the above quality) except those who are patient, and none is granted it except the owner of the great portion (of the happiness in the Hereafter i.e. Paradise and this world of a high moral character)."

[*Sūrah Fussilāt* 41:35]

Consider the following as an application of this matter. The Prophet (ﷺ) informed us how his people beat him up until he bled. He wiped the blood while saying,

اللَّهُمَّ اغْفِرْ لِقَوْمِي فَإِنَّهُمْ لَا يَعْلَمُونَ

THE NINTH MEASURE: TO SUPPRESS THE BLAZING FURY OF THE ENVIER

"O Allāh! Forgive my people as they do not know." [al-Bukhārī and Muslim]

The point is this measure is of a high caliber, and if the person successfully adopts it, he will be supported, safe, and protected by Allāh's permission.

TEN PREVENTIVE MEASURES AGAINST MAGIC AND ENVY

THE TENTH MEASURE: TO COMPLETELY PURIFY TAWHĪD FOR ALLĀH

To completely purify Tawhīd for Allāh and to believe that the means in this universe are the creation of Allāh; the Al-Mighty and Al-Wise. Also, one must know that none benefits nor harms except by Allāh's permission. Allāh says:

﴿ وَإِن يَمْسَسْكَ ٱللَّهُ بِضُرٍّ فَلَا كَاشِفَ لَهُۥ إِلَّا هُوَۖ وَإِن يُرِدْكَ بِخَيْرٍ فَلَا رَآدَّ لِفَضْلِهِۦ ﴾

THE TENTH MEASURE: TO COMPLETELY PURIFY TAWHĪD FOR ALLĀH

"And if Allāh touches you with adversity, there is none who can remove it but He; and if He intends any good for you, there is none who can repel His Favor, which He causes it to reach whomsoever of His servants He will. And He is the Oft-Forgiving, Most Merciful." [*Sūrah* Yūnus 10:107]

One should not overthink acquiring the means (of this life); instead, he should purify the Tawhīd for Allāh. We have mentioned before the saying of the Prophet (ﷺ),

وَاعْلَمْ أَنَّ الْأُمَّةَ لَوْ اجْتَمَعَتْ عَلَى أَنْ يَنْفَعُوكَ بِشَيْءٍ لَمْ يَنْفَعُوكَ إِلَّا بِشَيْءٍ قَدْ كَتَبَهُ اللهُ لَكَ، وَلَوْ اجْتَمَعُوا عَلَى أَنْ يَضُرُّوكَ بِشَيْءٍ لَمْ يَضُرُّوكَ بِشَيْءٍ قَدْ كَتَبَهُ اللهُ عَلَيْكَ.

TEN PREVENTIVE MEASURES AGAINST MAGIC AND ENVY

"And know that if the nation were to gather together to benefit you with anything, they would not benefit you except with what Allāh had already prescribed for you. And if they were to gather together to harm you with anything, they would not harm you except with what Allāh had already prescribed against you." [Recorded by al-Tirmidhi]

Ibn al-Qayyim said,

فَإِذَا جَرَّدَ الْعَبْدُ التَّوْحِيدَ فَقَدْ خَرَجَ مِنْ قَلْبِهِ خَوْفُ مَا سِوَى اللهِ ، وَ كَانَ عَدُوُّهُ أَهْوَن عَلَيْهِ مِنْ أَنْ يَخَافَهُ مَعَ اللهِ بَلْ يُفْرِدَ اللهَ بِالْمَخَافَةِ ... وَ يَرَى أَنْ إِعْمَالَهُ فَكره فِي أَمْرِ عَدَوِّهِ وَ خَوْفِهِ مِنْهُ وَاشْتِغَالَه بِهِ مِنْ نَقْصِ تَوْحِيدِهِ، وَ إِلَّا فَلَوْ جَرَّدَ

65 | Page

THE TENTH MEASURE: TO COMPLETELY PURIFY TAWHĪD FOR ALLĀH

تَوْحِيدَهُ لَكَانَ لَهُ فِيهِ شُغْلٌ شَاغِلٌ وَ اللهُ يَتَوَلَّى حِفْظَهُ وَ الدَّفْعُ عَنْهُ، فَإِنَّ اللهَ يُدَافِعُ عَنِ الَّذِينَ آمَنُوا، فَإِنْ كَانَ مُؤْمِناً فَاللهُ يُدَافِعُ عَنْهُ وَ لَا بُدَّ، وَ بِحَسَبِ إِيمَانِهِ يَكُونُ دِفَاعُ اللهِ عَنْهُ.

"Purifying the Tawhīd automatically renders the heart free of fear for anyone other than Allāh. At this point, one's enemy is too little to be feared. So, one should single out Allāh with fear. Furthermore, one should realize that worrying and fearing one's enemy is a sign of a defect in Tawhīd. Had one purified his Tawhīd, it would have preoccupied him from worrying about his enemy; since Allāh took care of his protection. Allāh defends those who believe; so, obviously, if he is a true believer, Allāh will

TEN PREVENTIVE MEASURES AGAINST MAGIC AND ENVY

certainly defend him. The extent to which Allāh defends the believer is solely dependent on how strong his faith is?"

You cannot help but notice now that the human being is in absolute need for strong faith, Tawhīd, and sincerity to Allāh in order to earn as much as possible of Allāh's aid. Ibn al-Qayyim continues,

وَ بِحَسَبِ إِيمَانِهِ يَكُونُ دِفَاعُ اللهِ عَنْهُ، فَإِذَا كَمَّلَ إِيمَانَهُ كَانَ دَفْعُ اللهِ عَنْهُ أَتَمَّ دَفْعٍ، وَ إِنْ مَزَجَ مُزِجَ لَهُ، وَ إِنْ كَانَ مَرَّةً وَ مَرَّةً فَاللهُ لَهُ مَرَّةً وَ مَرَّةً، كَمَا قَالَ بَعْضُ السَّلَفِ: مَنْ أَقْبَلَ عَلَى اللهِ بِكُلِّيَّتِهِ أَقْبَلَ اللهُ عَلَيْهِ جُمْلَةً، وَ مَنْ أَعْرَضَ عَنِ اللهِ

THE TENTH MEASURE: TO COMPLETELY PURIFY TAWHĪD FOR ALLĀH

بِكُلِّيَّتِهِ أَعْرَضَ اللهُ عَنْهُ جُمْلَةً، وَ مَنْ كَانَ مَرَّةً وَ مَرَّةً فَاللهُ لَهُ مَرَّةً وَ مَرَّةً.

"So, if one's faith in Allāh is perfect, Allāh's protection for him is equal to his faith, but if he were to mix up, it would be the same for Allāh's protection. Just like what some of the early scholars maintained, "Whoever seeks to go the distance closer to Allāh with his whole self (i.e. fully dedicated), Allāh will do the same for him, and conversely total negligence will result in total negligence from Allāh; and if it is a step by step forward, it will be the same from Allāh."

It all comes down to purifying Tawhīd and having strong faith and pure sincerity and resort to Allāh. "For this very cause, Tawhīd is Allāh's greatest invincible fortress, whose residents are guaranteed safety. Some of the Salaf said, "Whoever fears Allāh, everything will fear him; whereas who does not fear Allāh, Allāh will

TEN PREVENTIVE MEASURES AGAINST MAGIC AND ENVY

make him afraid of everything." A person who fears Allāh is rewarded by Allāh, as He makes people venerate him due to the prestige Allāh gives him. And indeed, everything in Allāh's hands.

To conclude, the measures mentioned above asserted by Ibn al-Qayyim are means that repel the evil of magic and envy. It requires from the truly guided believer to study them deliberately and strive to internalize and apply them. Eventually, he shall witness the pleasant consequences, good end, blessings, and safety in this life and the hereafter.

Allāh knows best; and may Allāh's peace and blessings be upon the servant of Allāh and Messenger, our Prophet Muhammad (ﷺ), his family, and his companions.

QUESTIONS

1- What is the ruling on hanging/wearing a bone, a cup, or something else to repel envy?

The answer: The Prophet (ﷺ) said,

مَنْ تَعَلَّقَ شَيْئًا وُكِلَ إِلَيْهِ

"Whoever hangs up something (as an amulet) will be entrusted to it."

And also,

إِنَّ الرُّقَى وَ التَّمَائِمَ وَ التِّوَلَةَ شِرْكٌ

"spells, charms and love potions are polytheism."

TEN PREVENTIVE MEASURES AGAINST MAGIC AND ENVY

Hanging/wearing items like those are enough reason for the person to be entrusted to them. So, what could be the outcome or the prize out of being entrusted to a bone hanged on the one's body?! Incidentally, the Prophet (ﷺ) saw a man with a brass ring on his hand. He said:

مَا هَذِهِ؟ قَالَ هَذِهِ مِنْ الْوَاهِنَةِ، قَالَ: انْزِعْهَا فَإِنَّهَا لَا تَزِيدُكَ إِلَّا وَهْنًا.

"What is this ring?" He said: "It is for Wāhinah." He said: "Take it off, for it will only increase you in weakness."

These items do not provide health benefits or protection against envy or anything for that matter. They rather weaken the human body more and more. Broadly speaking, wearing threads, amulets, bones, shells, or rings from gold, copper, metal or all other

QUESTIONS

items used for this particular activity is not only forbidden in the religion of Allāh but also a (type of) Shirk (polytheism). The question is whether it is major or minor Shirk. It actually depends on the person who wears them; if they are worn due to a belief that they would benefit or harm, such action is major Shirk that renders its doer out of the fold of Islam. But if they are worn due to a belief that they are merely a mean (to achieve personal need), such action is judged a minor Shirk because it is a medium leading to major Shirk.

The point is wearing these things are forbidden despite the different looks and shapes they take; some people wear or hang in his car an amulet with an eye engraved in it believing that it repels envy. Others hang one in the car in the shape of a hand with an eye drawn inside it. All of these superstitions done by the common people are due to their ignorance. They pin their hopes on things that neither harm nor benefit instead of

TEN PREVENTIVE MEASURES AGAINST MAGIC AND ENVY

pinning their hopes on Allāh, in whose Hands everything there is.

2- Should a funeral be held for the envier in order to suppress his envy and heal it? Does this have a proof?

The answer: No, it's baseless. The only cure is mentioned above in a beneficial scholarly manner by Ibn al-Qayyim.

3- A follow-up question: what does the Islāmic law permit regarding this issue?

If the envied person knows the envier, it is legitimate for the envied to use the same water in his ablution or shower used by the envier in his ablution or shower; or to sprinkle some of this water on himself. Such action is legitimate and authentically reported from the Messenger of Allāh.

QUESTIONS

4- Some people claim they interact with Muslim Jinni in order to break magical spells; is this permissible?

This is illegitimate. It is impermissible to make contact with Jinn even if they claim they're Muslims or otherwise because it is a door to evil. The legislative rule that maintain 'to nip evil in the bud before it grows into something bigger' is more than enough on this matter.

5- What is the preferable opinion in regards to reciting something while drinking the water in order to dispel magic and envy?

Reciting on the water and drinking, it is permissible, as it was recorded to have been done by some of the Salaf. It is better, however, to hold the recitation and the (gentle) water blowing on the afflicted (person) directly. It is also advisable that the afflicted is not to ask for Ruqyah. It is even better for him not to go to the

TEN PREVENTIVE MEASURES AGAINST MAGIC AND ENVY

person who would perform Ruqyah on him; but if he were to go, it would violate nothing but the perfection of his trust in Allāh; which is rather inadvisable. It is better for him in this situation to recite Ruqyah on himself, resort to Allāh, and push himself to be closer to Him, and observe the above instructions laid down by Ibn al-Qayyim.

6- Every time I engage myself in something, I feel that success is not my ally because of envy. Once, I bought a car but later had an accident; another time, I had a baby who died. This made me believe that envy is chasing me.

Sometimes, the person might be deluded into believing he is envied. He bases his belief on one or two incidents with having an already built-up idea they are because of envy. The questioner, if he were to disregard those two incidents and redirect his thinking towards his

QUESTIONS

other aspects of life, he would find himself living amidst multiple blessings. If he were to focus on his other life aspects apart from those two incidents and apart from the idea of envy, or even the delusion of one, he would conclude that his life is full of success and progress.

For instance, his very existence in this Masjid and attendance of this lecture is one of those successful life aspects Allāh blessed him with. Therefore, he should not single out those two incidents and jump to a conclusion that he is envied, and that it chases him wherever he goes. Some people blow things out of proportion, which sickens them. I advise him to disregard this delusion and to resort to Allāh instead; in addition, he should apply the earlier instructions by Ibn al-Qayyim, which is of critical importance.

7- How to protect the young against magic and envy?

TEN PREVENTIVE MEASURES AGAINST MAGIC AND ENVY

He should recite the following supplication, or his parents do it if he is incapable' "I seek protection in Allāh's perfect words from the evil of what He created." He could also use the Muawwizatin (i.e. Sūra al-Falaq, an-Nās), even if the child is not present, he should do so. The point is protecting children from such things is advisable. Also, one should accustom children to resort to Allāh and maintain regular remembrance of Him in the morning, night, and before sleeping.

8- **Recently, there has been an increasing number of T.V channels that promote magic; what is the ruling on watching them for the purpose of entertainment? Is there any advice for those who watch it?**

Watching those channels is prohibited, evil, and a mean for evil. A person who watches them is actually risking his religion. Needless to say the large number of people who critically suffered a serious damage in their religion because of similar (unnecessary) risk. The Salaf maintained, "If you were to risk with anything, never risk with your religion." Risk with your money or merchandise but never the religion. Many people care less for their religion enough to strangely risk it. They open all T.V channels and do not lock any. They watch them with no regard to the content they present. Likewise, the same goes for the internet websites.

Admittedly, this is a grave risk with the religion. Many youngsters fell for those channels and websites due to lack of knowledge and proper understanding, which led them to be victims of misconceptions that not only influenced their morals negatively but also their Aqeedah. Some of the corrupt doctrines of Christians and Jews along with others have crept into the minds of those youngsters, and it is because of risking the

TEN PREVENTIVE MEASURES AGAINST MAGIC AND ENVY

religion. Compare them to the Salaf; a man from the people of desire entered on Abdullah ibn al-Mubarak and offered to recite a verse from the Book of Allāh. Abdullah said: take him outside. The man insisted, "I want to recite a verse from the Book of Allāh before you." Abdullah replied: take him outside. After the man had left, those around Abdullah were wandering, 'he only wanted to recite a verse from the Book of Allāh!'

Abdullah replied, **"I was afraid he would throw a misconception at me that would stick to me until I die."** He is one of the most distinguished scholars of the successors, but he said something like this. How many misconceptions are available that baffle the minds of the youngsters because of watching those channels and logging into those websites. An unlimited number of misconceptions are so popular

QUESTIONS

and rampant. You may even notice that some of the questions presented before scholars are all misconceptions. Their form goes like this: O Shaykh; I'm hesitant between so and so, or I have a misconception.

Another number of people know large numbers of weak hadiths that have long settled in their hearts and filled their minds while being absolutely unaware and clueless of the beneficial knowledge. It is all because of risking the religion.

To conclude, watching those channels is impermissible, a sin, and a risk of one's religion. It is impermissible to watch them for the purpose of entertainment. As this is a waste of one's religion and engaging in what displeases Allāh. We ask Allāh to grant success, protection, and aid for everybody.

Made in the USA
Columbia, SC
30 April 2024